bul·ly
noun \bu̇-le

a blustering browbeating person; especially : one habitually cruel to others who are weaker

Come on, Matthew, let's head off to school.
My class is going to the lab to do something cool.

William, I don't want to. I really am scared.
There's a bully in my class and he just doesn't care.

When he beats up my friends or calls us all names.
He makes it no fun to play any games.

What's this bully's name; you tell your big brother.
I'll make sure this doesn't go any further.

No, William, don't do that. He'll just get all mad.
He grabs all our toys and talks really bad.

Now, Matthew, you know he's probably scared, too.
He may have no friends and takes it out on you.

Why don't you start by saying good morning to him.
And ask him to play with you and your friends.

If he still acts mean, then just tell him this:
You can't hurt me with your words or your fist.

I'm a big boy. I'm happy. I'm nice.
So before you're mean to me, you better think twice.

So off Matthew went to school that day.
With a knot in his stomach and a frown on his face.

He first saw the bully and started to turn.
And quickly remembered what he had just learned.

He said to the bully, you don't even know my name.
All you want to do is play this bullying game.

Well, not anymore. You can be my friend or not.
But you being mean to me just has to stop.

You could have some friends if you'd quit acting so mad.
There's me and Wood and our other friend Jack.

The bully got red and started to cry.

You're right. I'm lonely and really quite shy.

So off they went to find all their friends.
The bully said I'm sorry and wounds started to mend.

Matthew went home with a smile on his face.

William, he said, you were right today.

The bully was sad just like we discussed. He had no friends and took it out on us.

So we all had a little talk and worked it all out today.
And now we have a new friend to laugh with and play.

Remember, said William, don't let bullies hurt you.
You tell me, your teacher, and mommy and daddy, too.

Stand up for yourself and always be strong.
The right way to act always beats out the wrong.

www.ingramcontent.com/pod-product-compliance
Lightning Source LLC
Chambersburg PA
CBHW042127040426
42450CB00002B/107